# SHIVA

For Our Parents

With thanks to our teachers and all the yogis who made
this possible, especially Mahant Nagendra Giri
and Omkar Giri.

Also thanks to Jim Tomecko, Pushpa Tulachan, Sonja
Sherpa, Dubby Bhagat, Purna Giri, Laura Fouce,
Ashutosh Kasliwal, Sridhar Rana, Richard Seaman
and George Farrow.

Paula Fouce and Denise Tomecko;
**SHIVA**

Copyright 1990

**The Tamarind Press**

GPO Box 1996,
Bangkok,
Thailand.

Produced in Thailand.
Colour Separations by 71 Film.
Printed by Siriwattana Printing.

ISBN: 974-86974 - 3 - 6

# SHIVA

Text and Photos
by
**Paula Fouce**
**Denise Tomecko**

The Tamarind Press          Editions du Tamarinier

Bangkok   1990

# CONTENTS

# CHAPTER
# I
## THE BACKGROUND

*Shiva, the diligent young ascetic, personifies the ideal toward which all aspirants strive. He lives high in the Himalayas, removed from worldly concerns, free from desire and attachment - He is the perfected, self-realized yogi, depicted in meditation (**left**). The Himalayas remain a focus of Shiva worship with many shrines there, like this on a remote mountain (**right**).*

The earliest evidence of the origin of Lord Shiva came from the excavation of two ancient cities of the Indus civilization, Mohenjo-Daro and Harappa, which flourished between 2,000-3,000 years B.C. A large number of terra-cotta seals and statuettes were discovered in the region, providing a wealth of insight into the religious beliefs of the area. Among the seals were representations of a figure seated in a cross-legged position, similar to that of the Indian yogi; in many of the figurines he is depicted having three faces, and surrounded by animals.

Without a doubt he is the forerunner of the Hindu God Shiva - the Prince of Yogis, Lord of the Three Worlds, and Protector of Animals.

Also discovered were statues of a female figure, frequently seen with crops issuing from her womb. She was extensively worshipped as the Mother Goddess, the source of all fertility. Besides the two major deities, phallic symbols were revered. Emphasizing the creative power of nature, these later became associated with the generative power of Shiva Himself. There was also veneration of a sacred tree which later developed into worship of the peepal, the holy tree of the Hindus.

It seems that the religious practices of the Indus Valley were mostly performed in the home, as no temple buildings of any kind were discovered. Much about the religious ideology of these people is unknown, as the unusual script found there has not

*Posters are found all over India depicting Shiva in his various exploits, often in triumph over evil. Here He is portrayed saving a sinful hunter from the evil Lord Yama at the moment of death, because he had unconciously worshipped the linga in an all-night vigil.*

yet been deciphered.

This great Indus civilization came to an end around 1,500 B.C., with the invasion of Nordic Aryans who imposed their culture, beliefs, and Sanskrit language on the earlier Dravideans. At the time of the invasion the religious ideologies of the Aryans and Dravideans differed considerably.

Outside the Indus Valley, throughout the rest of India, a village life style was common. In this agricultural economy the value of the fertile earth and her products gave birth to worship of the Mother Goddess who is still idolized today in the Dravidean areas of South India. This worship was not characteristic of the invading Aryans, whose gods were almost entirely male.

Another feature of indigenous Indian religious belief is the law of karma, cause and effect, which determines man's destiny through many lifetimes. This belief, as well as veneration of a female deity, was later adopted by the Aryan invaders. What is known of the Aryans is mostly from their ancient collection of chants and hymns, called the 'Rg-Veda', written in the Vedic language, an earlier form of Sanskrit.

The Aryans believed that those who sinned were banished by the god Varuna, the dealer of justice and retribution, to a dismal place under the earth called "The House of Clay," while the pious went to the blissful "World of the Fathers."

Another important Vedic deity was Agni, the

*Parvati and Ganesh worship Shiva as the Linga or source of creation.*

fire god who accepted and took offerings to heaven for the gods. Later, when the Indo-Aryans cremated their dead, Agni was regarded as the one who transported mortal man to heaven after death.

The elite class of Aryan priests, Brahmins, gradually became accepted as the intermediaries between men and gods and co-operated with Agni in the performance of all sacrificial rituals, as offerings to the gods were always made through them.

Gradually the concept of karma was accepted as the Aryans became Dravideanized. The god Varuna yielded to Indra, god of war, who was of great importance to the Aryan warriors. The further migration into India by the Aryans brought many changes to the local cultural and religious attitudes including their Vedic social structure which divided people into religious, military, and economic communities. This hierarchy later developed into the caste system of India.

By the beginning of the Christian era modern Hinduism had become recognizable. In the intervening centuries Brahmanization of the local village cultures increased and the caste system developed.

Using the existing doctrine of karma to rationalize people's superior and inferior status, the Brahmins multiplied the numbers of existing classes and assigned them specific roles within the society.

The Brahmins felt their privileged position was being threatened by the growing affluence of the merchants and with the advent of Buddhism were at a further disadvantage, as the Buddha openly criticized their sacrificial rites for the unnecessary killing of animals.

The Buddhist prohibition of meat eating gradually spread and became a prominent feature of Hinduism, so the adaptable Brahmins downplayed their sacrifices and emphasized their role as educators and preservers of culture. Knowledge of Sanskrit was the closely guarded privilege of the Brahmins, and to gain influence with the newly rich merchant classes, they gave Sanskrit names to their village gods and invented new religious rites for them.

*Shiva's role in the pantheon of Gods has evolved from the Lord of Destruction in ancient times to a many faceted one today that also attributes him with, amongst other powers, that of procreation. Depicted here as the Young Ascetic, He carries a number of His varied symbols.*

The Brahmins preserved local customs and furnished myths and legends to assimiliate the elemental gods respectfully into their new pantheon.

They universalized the regional gods and soon a trinity emerged: Brahma, the Creator; Vishnu, the Preserver; and Shiva, the Destroyer. As Lord Brahma's importance gradually faded, Vishnu and Shiva became more popular. The Brahmins established themselves through determination to retain their status, religious tolerance and by imposing the caste system.

By the time of the Gupta Dynasty, 320-650 A.D., Shiva had become a God of love who also had a dark side, which he probably inherited from the Vedic god, Indra, the Lord of Destruction. Shiva was attributed with destroying the world at the end of each Kalpa, Hindu era. He became popular as the great ascetic whose meditation keeps the world in existence, and as the protector of animals. Also loved as the Lord of Procreation, His symbol became the linga, the male reproductive organ.

Goddess cults became popular in association with deities as their consorts. Shiva's consort became known as Parvati, Shakti, or Kali, and per-

*Together with Brahma the creator and Shiva the destroyer, Vishnu, the preserver, completes the holy trinity. In a temple on the outskirts of Kathmandu, a sleeping Vishnu is garlanded with floral offerings.*

sonified the divine power of femininity. Usually the consorts of gods were honoured by those who worshipped the male deity, but the Shaktas honoured the goddess as the principle deity. This was a revival of the earlier Dravidian mother goddess worship. It was believed that the goddess of nature creates only to destroy her creation, so she was regarded as a fierce, ruthless deity who needed to be appeased by offerings of life, both animal and human.

Human sacrifice became illegal in 1835 and the practice only survives nowadays in the form of animal sacrifice. During the British rule of India many of the cults went underground and became veiled in secrecy.

Thus the villagers actually managed to preserve their non-Brahmin gods under new names. While publicly acknowledging the importance of the Vedas and Brahmins, they worshipped their traditional deities as they always had. Over thousands of years the glorification of Shiva and his consort continued to flourish, expressing the basic human need to identify with higher spiritual forces.

Based on the findings at Mohenjo-Daro and Harappa, Shiva is probably the oldest of the known gods to whom homage is still paid by millions, emphasizing the endurance of the civilization which gave him birth and the timeless truths that have sustained him through the ages.

# CHAPTER
# II
# IN THE BEGINNING

Thousands of years ago, as history dawned in the distant Himalayas, there lived a few renunciants seeking to understand the mysteries of life. Aware of the transitory nature of existence, they sought lasting fulfillment by emulating their God, Rudra, Lord of the Wind, whose abode upon the summit of

*As Lakulisha, the bestower of wishes, Shiva is depicted with penis erect. Barren women with faith in His procreative power rub vermillion powder on His swollen phallus in the hope of becomming fertile.*

Mount Kailash, now in Tibet, has been sacred to Hindus throughout the ages. These long-haired ascetics lived apart from society, chanting and meditating to attain union with their Lord.

Dressing in black with rams' hides thrown over their shoulders, they shunned possessions by constantly wandering from place to place. They were said to be men who never die, who possessed magical powers and could see heaven from their lofty mountain retreats. Keeping their knowledge sacred, it was passed on by word of mouth from master to initiate and has come down through the ages in the form of stories, songs and legends.

*There is a tale in the 'Vishnu Purana,' a Hindu scripture, in which Brahma, the Lord of Crea-tion, conceived a child of blue complexion. When the new born baby began to cry, Brahma named him Rudra, "rud" means crying in Sanskrit. As his son continued to weep, Brahma tried to pacify him by giving the infant other names which he might prefer, such as Shiva, Shankara, Pashupati and Shambu. The name by which he became popularly known is Shiva.*

As he grew to manhood, Shiva played various roles in the world to demonstrate man's union with the Divine. He is generally portrayed in four ways:

The Young Ascetic
The Cosmic Dancer
The Lord of Destruction
The Wrathful Bhairab.

# CHAPTER
# III
## HIS MANIFESTATIONS

*A stone relief carving in Mahabalipuram, South India, of an ascetic practising a yoga posture in which he stands on one leg for prolonged periods of time.*

### "The Young Ascetic"

As an ascetic, Shiva has overcome the joys and sorrows of this finite world. Eternally youthful, He is of pale blue complexion, possessing a face so exquisitely beautiful that He appears both male and female. His long matted hair is worn in a massive topknot from which Mother Ganges flows down as the sacred river of India.

Atop His head is the crescent moon shining with the first radiance of creation. In the centre of His forehead is the third eye, the eye of wisdom, which destroys illusion and passion. Across His forehead and on other parts of His body are the triple lines of ash reminding us of the three impurities: egotism; *karma*, action with attachment to its fruits; and *maya*, illusion.

Bhairab's Dancers

*Groups of Bhairab's Dancers wander through the bazaars of India playing music and dancing Shiva's dance of grief while seeking alms (**above**). Imitating His elaborate costume a young boy dresses as the Ascetic Shiva, anticipating alms from passers-by (**below**).*

He carries a trident, *trishul,* representing the Hindu trinity of Brahma, the Creator; Vishnu, the Preserver; and Shiva, the Destroyer. In His other hand He plays a two-sided finger drum, *damaru,* merging His masculine and feminine aspects. His body is adorned with garlands of snakes, symbolizing His fearlessness and immortality.

*According to one legend, the wives of the great Rishis, or Saints fell in love with the hand-some young Shiva. The Rishis were jealous and angry, so they sent a tiger to kill Him. Shiva tore off the tiger's skin with His bare hands and used it as a meditation seat.*

*A snake was later sent to poison Him, but He subdued it and used the serpent as a necklace. Finally, they sent a terrifying demon to overpower Him, but Shiva quickly vanquished the demon and danced His fearful dance of victory over the body. When the Rishis, gods, celestial beings and demons saw His awesome dance of power, they realized His great supremacy and became His followers.*

16

*Hidden in the dark recesses of one of the oldest Shiva temples in Nepal is an antiquated wood carving of Bhairab. He stands, weapons in hand, displaying His power and masculinity. Erotic statues of Bhairab can frequently be found in temples to Shiva but are only exposed for occasional tantric rituals.*

## The Cosmic Dancer

As *Nataraja,* the Lord of Dance, Shiva commands the order and movement of the entire universe. He choreographs the drama played out on the earthly plane. His movements create the diverse images of life, ever-changing as He spins and whirls through time and space. Shiva Nataraja is constantly subjecting us to joy and sorrow, pleasure and pain. Ultimately He dominates all that lives, by dealing the hand of death.

In the *Tandava* dance of the victor over evil, Shiva Nataraja exhibits a fearful display of His cosmic energies, dancing in a circle of flames to the rhythm of universal motion. Balanced on one foot, He stands on the dwarf of ignorance with the careless abandon of one transported by His own music. His other foot is raised in the dancing pose, leading the way out of suffering. Nataraja has four arms: His left hand contains a ball of flames, fore-

*Two images in stone of Shiva's incarnation as 'Nataraj', the Cosmic Dancer who choreographs all order and movement in the universe.*

warning of the world's destruction and beginning anew the process of creation. His lower right hand is in the teaching pose, offering an end to eternal suffering through His grace. Pointing downward, His left hand expresses the final release from ignorance.

For centuries the myths and legends of Shiva and other gods were performed in temples and homes of devotees. These dramas gradually developed into the classical dance forms of India, such as *Bharatanatyam,* which capture the essence of Shiva in highly specialized movements and take years of study to perfect.

### The Destroyer

Shiva, the Lord of Destruction reigns over the dark forces of life and nature. The name Shiva itself comes from the root "sava," meaning corpse, characterizing His identification with death. The cycle of existence ever repeats the essential processes of birth, life, and death; whose counterparts in the Hindu trinity are Brahma the Creator, Vishnu the Preserver and Shiva the Destroyer.

As the great Destroyer, Shiva keeps the cycle of creation and destruction running its cosmic course. Without Him, the entire universe would cease to function, as creation can only rise from the ashes of destruction. Shiva is the great liberator, destroying the suffering and sins of mankind. He breaks down and dissolves all phenomena, releasing energy for further growth and transformation. He is death but He is also life.

### The Wrathful Bhairab

One of Lord Shiva's countless manifestations is the terrifying god Bhairab. Whenever retribution is to be dealt out, Shiva calls on Bhairab to ensure that justice is done.

*On one occasion Shiva wanted to punish Lord Brahma, who had been lusting after his own daughter. Brahma was so obsessed with her that he had sprouted heads in the four directions so that he could watch*

*Two of Bhairab's Dancers (**left**) replete with gaudily painted faces and costumes, perform in the streets for alms. All over India followers of Lord Shiva imitate and worship his varied incarnations, but all come together at the Kumbh Mela festival (**above**).*

*her wherever she went. Finally his daughter took refuge in the heavens, and when Brahma produced a fifth head to watch her there, Shiva was so angry that He created Bhairab and sent him to cut off Brahma's fifth head.*

*As punishment for the sin of killing a Brahmin, Bhairab was forced to wander the universe in agonizing grief, carrying the skull of Brahma in one hand. He was haunted by his crime until he cleansed himself of the horrible deed by bathing in a sacred pool in Varanasi.*

Many people believe that it is necessary to placate Bhairab to subdue his wrath, and some perform blood sacrifices of goats, chickens, and buffalo at his altars to appease him. Animal sacrifice is especially prevalent in northern India and Nepal.

As Bhairab is well known for his indulgence in intoxicants, certain sects of yogis invoke him while drinking alcohol and smoking hashish. Thus they identify more closely with the character of the terrifying god they emulate. They believe that Bhairab dwells in the cremation grounds in the form of wild dogs who scavenge their daily fare from the charred remains of human corpses.

Some of Bhairab's disciples imitate his dance of grief whilst begging. Dressing up in their colourful attire takes hours as they put on multicoloured rags, myriads of bells, rosary beads, and ash. The effect is completed by the ritualistic wrapping of yards of wool cord around their waists, spun by *yogis* trained in the time consuming art. As they wend their way through the bazaars dancing, they announce their arrival by shouting, *''Alag, bom, bom, bom !''* Great spirals of incense smoke rise into the air from the gigantic coconut shells which serve as their begging bowls.

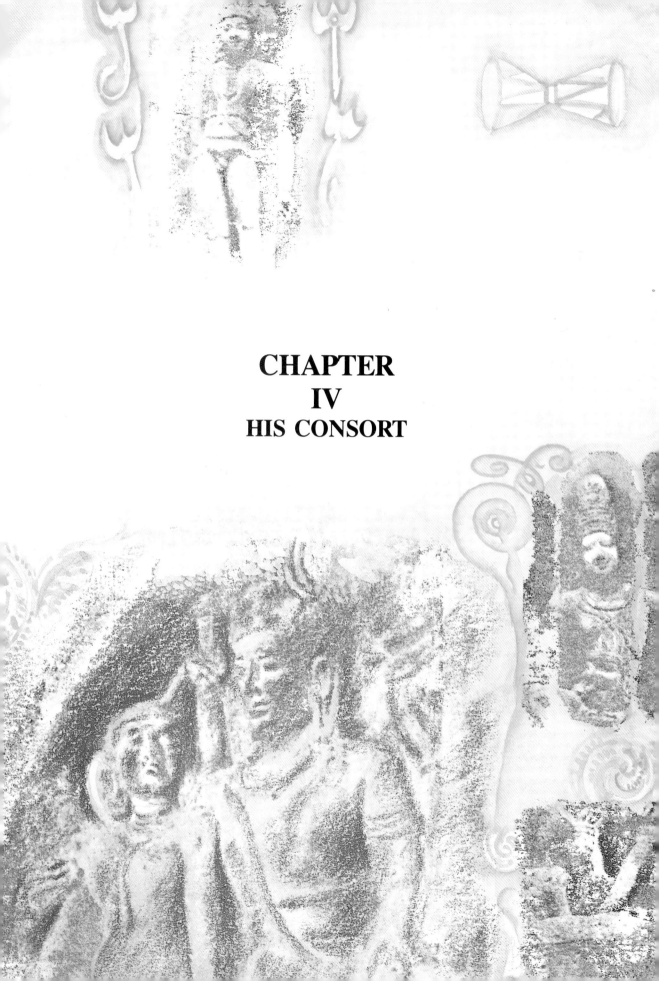

# CHAPTER
# IV
## HIS CONSORT

*The hands of Shiva's wife, Sati, carved in stone.*

Although Shiva is worshipped as the ruler of the three worlds and the strongest of the gods, His power, or *Shakti*, is represented by his wife or consort. Together they fulfill a parental role, ministering to the needs of mankind.

The story of Shiva's first wife Sati is the subject of a tale from the *'Swasthani,'* an ancient Sanskrit text, which is a collection of myths recounting the escapades of Shiva and His friends. It is also a medium through which many young people are introduced to sex; the tales are both social and religious, and are written in an amusing manner.

*Shiva had married the exquisite young Sati against the wishes of her father, Daksha. It was only through a trick, and the help of Lord Vishnu, that Shiva had managed to win her as His wife. Daksha found Shiva's appearance and manners revolting and did not feel He was a suitable match for his favorite daughter. Daksha's other daughters were all married to distinguished gods, so when Daksha decided to hold a feast and fire sacrifice, he invited all his daughters, sons-in-law and other important guests, with the exception of Shiva and Sati.*

*On the day of the feast the cosmic prankster, Narada, was surprised to find that Shiva and Sati were not attending, and fearing some misfortune may beset the ritual sacrifice without the Lord of Destruction present, he quickly set off for Mount Kailash to call Shiva. There he informed them of the feast and the fact that they had not been invited.*

*Shiva was hardly surprised by the news and remained indifferent, but Sati was deeply hurt by the direct insult to her husband and by her father's rejection of them both. Sati insisted on going to the feast to speak to her father and she left Kailash with Narada. When Sati questioned her father about his unbearable insult, he said that while he had nothing against her, he could not stand the sight of her husband and had no intention of inviting Him to such a distinguished gathering. Sati was devastated at her father's harsh words and threw herself on the sacrificial fire crying, "Shiva, Shiva."*

*The guests were horrified at Sati's demise and Narada flew to Kailash to tell Shiva what had happened. Hearing the news, Shiva's sorrow knew no bounds, He pulled a hair from His head and threw it on the ground. It caused an explosion in the*

*Shiva's divine family is exquisitely portrayed on this brass doorway at Gokarna, Nepal. He and His sensuous wife Parvati are enthroned in the centre. To the left is their beloved son Ganesh, the bestower of wisdom, much revered in the Hindu pantheon. On the right is Kartikeya their second son, commander of Shiva's mighty army.*

*This stone carved relief on a temple wall in Udaipur, shows the divine couple Shiva and Parvati entwined in a playful embrace.*

midst of which the wrathful goddess Kali appeared with a retinue of demons, and asked of what service she could be to Shiva. He then threw down another hair and Bhairab materialized carrying a mighty trident. Shiva ordered them to go at once to kill Daksha, destroy the sacrifice and create havoc among the gods.

A huge battle took place at the scene of the ill-fated feast and everyone withdrew realizing Shiva's incomparable power. Bhairab then cut off Daksha's head and threw it on to the sacrificial fire. When Daksha's wife saw this she begged him to restore her husband and sole protector to life. Bhairab compassionately responded to her plea, and taking the head of the sacrificial goat, placed it on Daksha's body back to front, so that people would always see how ignorant and stupid he had been.

The two wrathful manifestations then returned to Kailash giving Shiva a full account of the events. Shiva was pleased and reabsorbed them into His own body and went to Daksha's home. When He saw Satı lying dead amid the flames He was desolate. Since Agni, the fire god, had not consumed Sati's body for fear of Shiva's wrath, the body was still intact; Shiva lifted it across His shoulders and wandered aimlessly around the world. Sati's body did not decompose and the gods took pity on Shiva's endless grief. They asked Vishnu to do something to help, so Vishnu invented the fly, which caused the body to rot, and as it broke apart, fragments of the corpse fell in fifty places throughout India and Nepal, sanctifying them forever.

The most revered shrines of Hinduism have evolved where the pieces of Sati's body fell; her tongue fell in Kashmir, her head in Varanasi and her female organ, "yoni" in the Kathmandu Valley of Nepal.

Sati, in her perfect love and devotion to Shiva, soon took rebirth to be with Him again in a second and more enduring relationship. The ever playful Narada noticed Parvati on one of his journeys and found her to be the epitome of sensual beauty. Narada was so impressed that he went directly to Vishnu to suggest a marriage between them.

When Vishnu had heard his description, he was convinced of her charms and immediately sent Narada to Parvati's father to make the necessary arrangements. Her father was flattered that a god of Vishnu's stature wanted his daughter as a wife, and he quickly agreed to fix an auspicious day for the ceremony.

At the appointed time Vishnu arrived with his entourage, but Parvati, who since her childhood had always prayed to have Shiva as her husband, ran away and hid in the forest leaving Vishnu and the rest of her family in embarrassed confusion. From her hiding place Parvati fervently beseeched Lord Shiva to come to her aid.

Shiva was impressed with her supplications and appeared before her asking what He could do. She begged Him to take her as His wife, but Shiva recalling the unfortunate circumstances surrounding His previous marriage said that He would only do so with the consent of her father. He then advised her to go to Vishnu and put the matter before him. When Vishnu had listened to Parvati's entreaties he gave her certain practices to perform and his consent, ensuring her that her father would also agree if she could persuade Shiva to remarry again.

To encourage the match, Kama, the god of desire, was sent to shoot his magic arrow into Shiva's heart. Unfortunately for Kama his action disturbed Shiva's deep meditation, and upon waking He unleashed the destructive power of His third eye sending out a shaft of fire that left Kama in a smoldering pile of ashes.

But Kama's mission had been completed, and when Shiva returned to His meditation He realized that Sati, His first wife, had been reborn as Parvati and longed for the union to be complete once again. Before making a final decision He decided to put Parvati to a test, and appeared before her as Indra, Lord of the gods, telling her that Shiva was a worthless mad yogi and begging her to marry him instead.

This enraged Parvati and she started to curse him. Suddenly Shiva changed into His true form and told her how pleased He was with her constance. They then went happily to her father to obtain his formal consent and make the final arrangements for the wedding.

*Durga depicted killing The Demon of Ignorance*

# CHAPTER
## V
### HIS SONS

*Shiva's wife Parvati, with their son Ganesh.*

## Ganesh

Ganesh, the remover of obstacles, is the son of Shiva and Parvati. One of the most beloved deities in the Hindu pantheon is the elephant-headed god Ganesh, who is worshipped first in all Hindu rituals, as he is the harbinger of good fortune and the lord of wisdom. There is a popular story describing how he came to have an elephant's head on a plump human body.

*Parvati was alone in the forest awaiting Shiva's return from a long retreat. Not knowing when He would come, she decided to create a son. Before*

*Natural formations which resemble deities are frequently worshipped, such as this abstract stone image of Ganesh.*

beginning her daily bath, she formed Ganesh from the dust on her body. She gave her young son the task of guarding her bathing place, to ward off any intruders who might disturb her privacy. Shiva arrived back unexpectedly, and wishing to see Parvati immediately went to the bathing place. Here He was denied entry by Ganesh, who had never seen his father. Shiva was furious at being prevented from seeing His wife, and not knowing Ganesh was His son, cut off the boy's head.

When Parvati saw what had happened she was broken-hearted and begged Shiva to restore their son to life. Shiva, realizing His mistake sent His guards off in all directions telling them to bring back the head of the first creature they found. One of the guards saw a beautiful white elephant and brought the head to Shiva who placed it on His son's body redeeming his life.

Ganesh is not only the bestower of boons but also personifies the virtues of a balanced life. He demonstrates that opposites such as the enormous elephant and the tiny rat, who is his vehicle, can live together happily, and that the love of good food and profound spiritual knowledge can also be combined. He testifies that the world is full of opposites which co-exist peacefully side by side.

### Kartikeya

All of Shiva's offspring had extraordinary births and the arrival of Kartikeya, His second son, was no exception.

After marriage, Shiva and Parvati shut themselves in their room, enjoying each other's company so much that they neglected their duties to mankind. Indra, in an effort to stimulate their greater participation in human affairs sent Agni, the god of fire, to find out what was amiss.

When Agni arrived he was stopped at the gate by Shiva's guards, who told him that he could not enter. Not to be put off so easily, Agni vaporized

*Kartikeya, his mount a peacock, is son of Lord Shiva and Mother Ganges*

himself, entered the room through a crack, and then rematerialized as a mendicant begging for alms.

Although Agni hid his shock at seeing Shiva and Parvati locked in loving embrace, Shiva became so angry at the interruption, He almost destroyed Agni on the spot. Had it not been for the intervention of Parvati who reasoned that no good could come of killing Agni, He would surely have met his

end. Parvati asked Shiva to give him alms so that he would go away, whereupon Shiva scooped up His sperm and gave it to him. Agni didn't know what to do with it, so swallowed the offering and left.

Fearing that he might become pregnant, Agni stopped on the banks of the Ganges and spewed the sperm onto the grass, returning empty handed to Indra. Meanwhile in the spot where Agni had left

*Ganesh in a particularly resplendent, large bronze alloy.*

the sperm, a fire began to burn, and when the wives of the Rishis, six saints, were returning home from their daily bath, they stopped to warm themselves by the fire.

Much to their surprise these women became pregnant, and as they were unable to offer a reasonable explanation to their husbands, they were cursed and banished. As the wives passed by the Ganges they vomited the sperm into her waters, and ascended as bright stars into the heavens, becoming the Pleidaes constellation.

Out of the Ganges Kartikeya was born, son of Mother Ganges and Shiva, the Lord of the Three Worlds. When he grew to manhood, Kartikeya became the commander of Lord Shiva's army, his mount a colorful peacock.

# CHAPTER
# VI
## HIS VEHICLE

Each member of the Trinity has an animal who acts as his vehicle. Shiva's mount is the beautiful milky white bull, Nandi, who is enormous with powerful red-tipped horns and large, loving eyes.

This magnificent animal was presented to Shiva by His father-in-law, Daksha, as a marriage gift, and was named Nandi which means "giving joy." He embodies the power that can be attained through the taming of strength and fierceness. Shiva rides on the back of Nandi, as only those who have mastered desire and gained self-knowledge can ride the blissful bull.

In India, many bulls are allowed to roam about freely and graze wherever they please. These large animals are worshipped by the devout who touch their backs in reverence to receive their blessing and are sometimes branded with the sign of the trident. Upon death sacred bulls are given great funeral rites in recognition of their likeness to Nandi, Shiva's vehicle.

*The powerful white bull, Nandi, is Shiva's mount. He is seen paying homage at the doorway of a Shiva temple in Mahabalipuram, South India.*

# CHAPTER
# VII
## HIS SYMBOLS

*Shiva's most worshipped symbol, the Linga, is surrounded by His portrait, his mount Nandi and other symbols (right). Holy sites throughout India, particularly unusual geographic formations in the Himalayas, are adorned with Shiva's symbols left by worshippers (overleaf).*

*The trident, two-sided drum and serpent shaped horn are often carried by Shiva yogis, as a reminder of their spiritual quest.*

Many symbols have come to be associated with Lord Shiva and although their origins are obscured by time, their meanings are as true and vibrant as ever.

In Hindu mythology, as in many cultures, snakes are considered a sign of mystical and sexual power. The garlands of serpents, *naga,* worn around Lord Shiva's neck represent the phallus or *linga.* So strong is the belief in its power that barren women worship Shiva's erect penis and those who dream of serpents, believe they will conceive. Devotees

also rub red vermilion powder onto the erect penis of Shiva Lakulisha, the giver of wishes, to overcome infertility. Throughout the entire subcontinent, all varieties of phallic shapes symbolize Shiva.

Ever present at Shiva's side is a *trishul,* trident, signifying His mastery over the three qualities of Nature, the *gunas:* wisdom and purity, stimulation and passion, inertia and impurity. These three attributes bind man to the illusory world, or *Maya.* Shiva Himself is known to have overcome the three gunas, and is in a perfect state of equilibrium. The

trident also embodies the three aspects of the Hindu trinity: Lords Brahma the Creator; Vishnu the Preserver; and Shiva the Destroyer, and the vertical structure of the *trishul* connects heaven and earth, bridging the gap between devotees and their Lord.

As Shiva yogis constantly wander from one pilgrimage place to another, they carry only a few possessions, one of which is an enormous trident. When a *yogi* reaches a place sacred to Shiva, he drives his valued *trishul* into the earth, leaving it as a permanent offering to His omnipresence.

The *damaru* is a two-sided finger drum indicating the masculine and feminine aspects of nature. The male aspect Shiva, and the female *Shakti,* are joined in divine embrace. Another symbol of this male-female union is the *Sri Yantra* mandala, a geometric form made up of two superimposed triangles; the upturned being the phallus of Shiva while the inverted one is the vagina or *yoni,* representing Shiva's consort the sensuous goddess Parvati. The three horizontal lines He wears on His forehead are *Tripundaka.* These markings signify the three

syllables which make up the primordial vibration, A-U-M; the trident; and the three *gunas,* qualities of nature. The lines are generally made of ash from a holy fire or ground sandalwood paste, and are believed to cool the brain while meditating.

Shiva's matted locks are piled high, crowning His head and providing a cushion for the River Ganges to break her fall as she flows down from heaven to earth. He wears a crescent moon nestled in His hair, as it signifies His perfect control of the mind. The tiger is the symbol of lust and as the Lord has conquered His passions, He uses its skin as His seat.

Shiva's third eye shines with eternal wisdom which He bestows on His devotees. He wears a necklace of seeds from the Rudraksha tree, believed to be His tears fallen from heaven. Rudraksha seeds usually have five facets, sometimes more or less, the most valued being the one faceted seed. A strand of one hundred and eight rudraksha, believed to absorb negativity, is used as a rosary by devotees of Shiva, to recite His divine name.

# CHAPTER
# VIII
## HIS WORSHIP

*In reverence, offerings are brought for consecration to Shiva's holy shrine, then taken home and shared with other members of the family, bringing the sacredness of the temple into the home and daily life.*

Religion is an integral part of daily life in the Indian subcontinent, there is hardly a separation between worship and worldly affairs. People bow to sacred cows blocking the road, they pause to ring a temple bell while walking through the marketplace, offering coins to a beggar, and flowers to a shrine. Ceremonial rituals are performed virtually at any time, and nearly every home has a family altar where its members worship each day. Although this spirit runs through all aspects of Hindu culture and everything is considered sacred, some things are especially venerated in the worship of Lord Shiva.

Monday is dedicated to Shiva and devout women fast each week on this day in His honour. The Eastern lunar calendar is filled with religious festivals, based on the moon's phases, and each new moon is considered auspicious by His disciples since it is cherished by Shiva who wears it shining in His locks. A crescent moon which occurs on a Monday is extremely holy and is observed as Lord Shiva's day, as is every thirteenth of the month.

People pay homage to

*A tika of vermillion powder, on the forehead of a young girl, brings protection and blessings from the goddess Parvati. Tikas are made of consecrated powders, food or ash and applied during worship or religious rituals.*

images of Shiva and His *linga* by washing them with cow's milk and water from sacred rivers, such as the Ganges. They are annointed with clarified butter and sandalwood paste, and decorated with flowers and leaves of the *peepal* tree, sacred to Lord Shiva. Offerings of bel fruit and *dhatura,* an hallucinogen from which belladonna is extracted, are made as these gifts are loved and appreciated by the Lord.

    *Aarti,* the ritual offering of light, takes place each sunrise and sundown to awaken Shiva and put Him to rest. The *pujari,*

or priest, performs the ceremony and is in charge of the shrine, lovingly cleaning and caring for it. Incense is offered, and a metal dish containing flames from burning wicks is passed through the air before the *murti,* image, in a clockwise motion symbolizing the sun. Bells chime loudly, calling Shiva's attention and summoning His devotees to the temple. A whisk is waved around the image to purify the atmosphere. As the priest enacts the ancient rites, he turns to each of the four cardinal directions, flicking water from a conch shell,

*Aarti is performed at sunrise and sunset in Shiva temples,
offering water and fire in the four directions. Devotees
gather to sing prayers and pay homage to the gods. After
the ritual, people pass their hands over the flame and raising
them to their heads, receive the warmth of Shiva's blessing*

*Images of favoured gods are painted over village doorways, to ensure the inhabitants of protection by their chosen deity.*

*For the salvation of the dead, pilgrims walk for miles carrying an assortment of Shiva pictures, plastic toys and flowers, offering sacred Ganges water to all Shiva shrines en route.*

the symbol of purity. Afterwards the *aarti* prayer is sung, and people pass their hands over the sacred flames for *darshan,* blessing.

They return home with flower petals and other offerings from the ceremony, as blessings to be shared with members of the family. Thus the sense of sacredness is carried from the temple into the home and every aspect of daily life.

*Coloured powders, such as this vermillion, are sold for use in worship ceremonies. They are applied to the centre of the forehead to denote the wisdom eye and rubbed on to statues in devotion.*

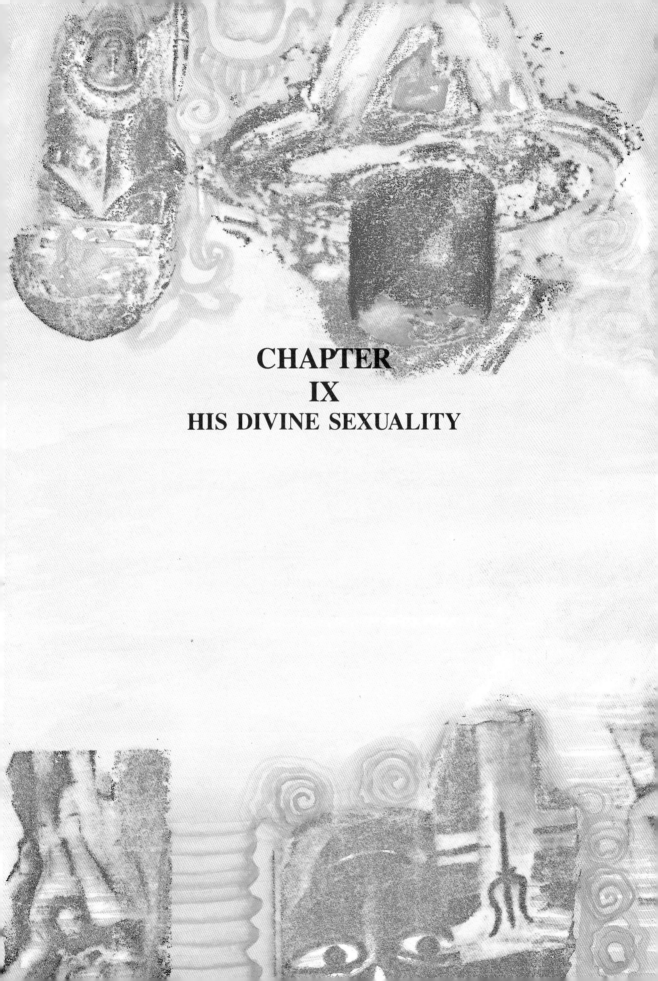

# CHAPTER
## IX
### HIS DIVINE SEXUALITY

The creative essence of Shiva is evident in the worship of the *linga*, phallus, and *yoni*, its female counterpart. The origin of this worship is related in the *'Linga Purana'*.

*Lords Brahma, Vishnu and Vasishta went to Mount Kailash, the abode of Shiva, to pay their respects to Him. They happened to arrive in the midst of Shiva and Parvati's lovemaking.*

*Shiva had been drinking and was so preoccupied that he did not realize his indecency. Vishnu could not help laughing at the sight of their uncontrolled passion, but the other gods were deeply insulted. They shouted angrily, "Let no decent person have any association with you," and having cursed him they left.*

*As the couple slowly came out of their reverie Shiva asked his guards who had intruded. When the guards recounted the visitation of the gods and the anger with which they had departed, the words fell so heavily on Shiva's and Parvati's ears that they died of humiliation in their position of lovemaking.*

*Shiva wished that the act which had caused them so much shame should be remembered forever by all mankind. He said, "I am the supreme being and so is my linga; all who worship; it as a god will receive their place in Kailash." Their shame killed Shiva and Parvati but also gave them eternal life in the form of the linga and yoni.*

The *linga*, fountain of life, is shown in its erect form with its top pointing upwards and is usually placed in the *yoni*. It is one of the oldest symbols

*By setting a slow-dripping bowl above this linga (**left**), one worshipper has significantly extended his period of devotion.*

*A Shiva linga survives for worship (**above**) while it's temple in Gorkarna, Nepal, crumbles.*

*The combination of linga and it's embracing yoni, like the union of man and woman, represents the creative seed and it's nurturing womb - the source from which all life springs in eternal enjoyment.*

worshipped throughout the Hindu world.

Originally the cylindrical shape represented the formlessness of creation and only gradually became associated with Lord Shiva. There is no representation of Shiva more sacred than the *linga*. The oldest *linga* in existence are the twelve *Jyoti-linga,* self-born or *adilinga.* Scattered across the Indian sub-continent, these ancient tributes were not manmade, but naturally formed. The world was created by the emission of Shiva's semen, so Shiva is represented as an erect phallus, perpetually virile but not yet consummated. The *linga* shows He has transcended sexual desire; He is the eternal and vigilant ascetic.

The *yoni* embraces the *linga* and is the source of all that exists, it manifests nature from which everything evolves. The creative seed and the nurturing womb are drawn together in enjoyment and the whole universe springs forth from the union.

# CHAPTER
# X
## HIS HOLY RIVER
## MOTHER GANGA

*Pilgrims bathe in the holy waters of the River Ganges at Hardwar.*

The River Ganges, more than all other rivers, has inspired the hearts of the Indian population through the Ages. The uncounted millions who have prayed on her banks and bathed in her waters from the source to the sea, tell the colourful story of India's spiritual quest.

In the *'Brahmavaivarta Purana'*, Shiva said of the Ganges: *"She is the source of redemption... Heaps of sin accumulated by a sinner during millions of births are destroyed by mere contact of a wind charged with her vapor... As fire consumes fuel, so this stream consumes the sins of the wicked."*

Not only is the Ganges said to cleanse both body and soul, but also to have unusual properties

*Bathing in the holy river Ganges is believed to absolve sin and ensure a higher rebirth in the Hindu cycle of birth, death and reincarnation.*

of self-purification. In the city of Varanasi thousands of people drink water directly from the township; yet it is surprisingly rare to hear of the kind of epidemics one might expect. Neither do the numerous partially cremated and rotting corpses floating in it seem to make its water a hazard to health. Hindus attribute this fact to the river's divine essence, which is eternally pure.

The source of India's holiest river is a particularly sacred pilgrimage place. Situated between craggy Himalayan peaks, the river bursts out of a glacier at Gaumukh, the cow's mouth, and rushes down towards Gangotri, the last resting place for pilgrims before the ascent to the source. Some people travel for months carrying bedding, cooking pots, offerings and religious books on the journey of a lifetime, the climax of which is the ultimate holy dip at Gaumukh.

En route to Gangotri pilgrims visit the Kedarnath glacier, the birthplace of Mahadakini, another sacred river which eventually joins with the Ganges,

and is also the site of one of the twelve great naturally formed *Jyoti linga,* famed throughout India. Yamnotri and Badrinath with its beautiful hot springs are visited in the same spirit of devotion.

About three hundred miles from its source, the Ganges breaks out of the Himalayan range and enters the Indian plain at the town of Hardwar, the gate of Shiva. Many holy men and revered saints live in the forests of the area.

For the devout, a visit to the four Dhams is considered essential to their religious life. these are Badrinath in the North, Rameshwaram in the South, Dwarka in the West and Puri in the East.

One can only admire the aged and infirmed pilgrims making their way resolutely step by step up the difficult mountain paths, chanting praises to the Lord. Staff in hand and a small bundle balanced on their heads, they leave their homes and families to realize the final aspiration: a visit to the four holiest places in India and a bath in the icy waters at the sacred source of Mother Ganga.

# CHAPTER
# XI
## 'SHIVA'S CITY OF LIGHT'

*Varanasi, or Benares, the holy city of Shiva on the Ganges, is said by some to be the oldest city on earth.*

Varanasi, built along the banks of the holy River Ganges, is the earthly dwelling place of Lord Shiva. Called Banares by the British, it was originally known as Kasi, the City of Light, and is said to be the oldest existing city on earth.

In the *'Shiva Purana'* it is written that Kasi is supported by Shiva's trident, and that it has the power to absorb and destroy man's negative Karma. It is the holy of holies of the Hindu world.

The aged and dying come to Varanasi to live out their remaining days until death, when they are cremated on the banks of the sacred river. To be cremated here ensures one of a positive rebirth in the cycle of reincarnation. Pilgrims from all over India bring the ashes of their loved ones to Kasi, scattering them into the hallowed river's water, in the belief that their sins will be cleansed.

Known as the "City of Burning and Learning," Varanasi is a cultural center of India, renowned for classical studies and music. The entire length of the Ganges is lined with bathing ghat, platforms, temples, and palaces built years ago by Maharajas from each state of India. *Pandit,* or priests do a swift business on the riverside dispensing blessings from their platforms, placing tika, marks on the foreheads of pilgrims signifying the third eye, and uttering the appropriately auspicious prayers.

Early each morning thousands of people make their way to the Ganges to salute the rising sun while immersed in the waters of salvation. The water is thick with floral offerings placed by pilgrims in reverence to the holy river. Following the bath, they walk through the colourful crowded bazaars along lanes

*Varanasi, built along the banks of the Ganges, is Hinduism's sacred capital. It is believed to be the oldest existing city on earth and Shiva's terrestrial abode. All devout Hindus hope to die here and have their ashes scattered on the river, purifying lifetimes of sin and promising a fortunate rebirth.*

that twist and turn to the most revered of temples - *Kasi Vishwanath*. Vendors fill the narrow streets hawking religious articles of every description. Nearby is the largest cremation *ghat* in India, where hundreds of bodies are consigned to the flames each day. A thick shroud of pungent smoke lies heavily in the air, its aroma tingeing the atmosphere with a constant reminder of human mortality and Shiva.

# CHAPTER
# XII
## SHIVA AND DEATH

*One of the last rites to be performed by the family is to place fragrant camphor into the mouth of the corpse and light it as an offering to the gods. The pyre is then ignited and straw scattered over the body to hide it from view during the cremation.*

Through His destruction, Shiva claims and regenerates life-death is His dominion. In a world dominated by a distorted vision of reality the thought of death and its consequences can be extremely disturbing. The direct experience of parting from all that one loves and cherishes and entering a completely different state of consciousness, is confusing and even frightening.

For the Hindu the possibility of a more or less fortunate rebirth is a major concern, due to their deep rooted belief in *karma* and the ancient caste system. Convinced that their past actions have caused them to be born into a particular caste, they hope that their good deeds will earn them a rebirth in a higher one, with less suffering in the material world.

The four castes of Indian society are *Brahmin, Kshatriya, Vaisya* and *Sudra.* The highest caste is the *Brahmin,* the priestly class, who perform all religious ceremonies, are the scholars and are supported by the community. All *Brahmins* wear a sacred thread, given to them by their *guru* in a ceremony somewhat like a Christian confirmation.

Second in the social order are the *Kshatriya,* the warriors, who defend and protect society. They are responsible for the implementation of justice and work as soldiers.

Third on the social ladder are the *Vaisya,* the business men and shopkeepers, who run the economy.

The lowest caste are the *Sudra,* sometimes called Untouchables, who were named the children of God or *Harijan* by Mahatma Gandhi. They are the laborers and servants, who perform the lowly jobs such as shoe mending and the handling of corpses.

The death rites of each caste and ethnic group are different, but follow a general pattern to which is added the special ceremonies of their sect.

The dead body is undressed and swaddled in cloth before being laid on a stretcher made of newly cut green bamboo. Wealthier families cover the body with a rich antique brocade cloth, which is kept for

*Wearing white, the colour of mourning, the eldest son of the family pays his last respects to his deceased father before completing the customary rituals and putting a torch to the funeral pyre. Around the father's head is wrapped his astrological chart, traditionally prepared at birth and finally burned with him at the completion of life.*

this ceremonial purpose by their caste, or extended family group. The male members of the clan then carry the body to the temple. Females very seldom attend cremations on account of their sensitive nature.

While the funeral pyre is prepared the body is laid on the steps, sometimes with its feet in the holy river, symbolizing the last ritual bath. Some people are taken to the temple just before death, so that they pass away with their feet in the river, cleansed of sin. When the pyre is constructed, the corpse is laid on it with the head facing east. Friends and relatives pay last respects to their loved one, while close family members touch their foreheads to the feet of the deceased in a final act of parting.

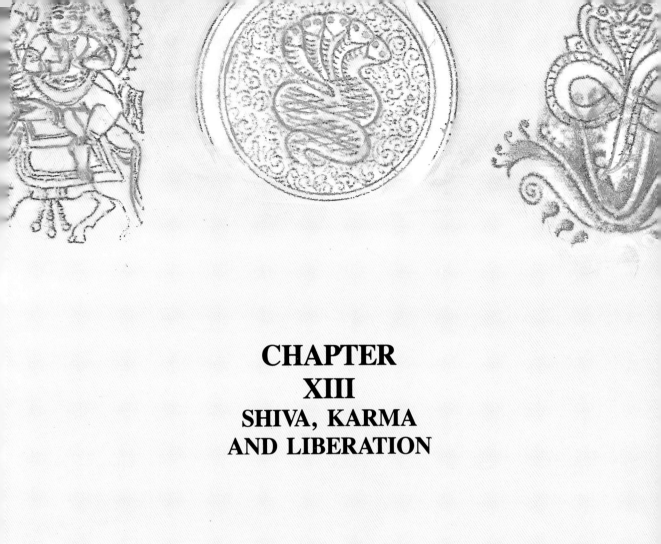

# CHAPTER
# XIII
## SHIVA, KARMA
## AND LIBERATION

*Businessmen stop at a temple to worship on their way to work while beggers linger on the steps hoping for alms. According to the law of karma, a person may be born wealthly or poor, influential or outcast, depending on the accumulated effects of his actions in previous lives.*

"As a man's desire is, so is his destiny. For as his desire is, so is his will, and as his will is, so is his deed, and as his deed is, so is his reward, whether good or bad."

**Brihadaranyaka Upanishad**

*Karma,* the law of cause and effect, is one of the oldest explanations of justice. What a man is in his present life has been determined by his past conduct, whilst his present conduct shapes the kind of life he will have in the future. This theory explains why some men appear to suffer misfortune undeservedly and why apparently bad people do not suffer any obvious retribution.

Although the theory of *karma* provided a moral code by which men could lead their lives, the Himalayan ascetics were not satisfied with this explanation

*During the Shiva Ratri vigil, a pratitioner meditates and repeats mantras while balancing a basin of red hot coals on his head. His face is shrouded with cloth to avoid distractions and to facilitate deeper concentration for meditation.*

*Outside the desert town of Jaisalmer, where the harsh dry landscape provides no river at which to burn the dead, stand the cremation platforms of Brahmins.*

*Even with its occupant gone, this temporory 'home' of a Shiva devotee is obvious due to the varied symbols.*

alone. They questioned predestination and the passive attitude of acceptance most Hindus had towards their fate. They felt that life, for better or worse, was essentially full of suffering, and that the only way out was to break the cycle of death and rebirth.

They renounced materialism, believing that the source of all suffering was *Maya,* the illusion that the transitory world was reality and that desires could be satisfied. They sought liberation from endless lifetimes of suffering, through renunciation of desire and by practicing asceticism and meditation, in emulation of their Lord.

They believed that when action was no longer prompted by desire, *karma* was not created and union with the Divine, Shiva, could be attained. This was a turning point in the history of Eastern religion, as these ideas gave an esoteric meaning to existence and a higher goal beyond the mundane.

*"He who lacks discrimination, whose mind is unsteady and whose heart is impure, never reaches the goal, but is born again and again. But he who has discrimination, whose mind is steady and whose heart is pure, reaches the goal and having reached it is born no more."*

One of the many ascetics who congregate at Varanasi meditates on the steps above Mother Ganges' waters.

# CHAPTER
# XIV
## KATHA UPANISHAD
## THE PATH TO SHIVA

*To develop the power of mind over matter, ardent practitioners endure many hardships on the path. This yogi will stand continuously on his feet for twelve years, leaning on a padded swing to sleep.*

**Y**oga means union of man with his Higher Self. It is an ancient discipline that can be traced back as far as the third century B.C., when the forest dwelling ascetics broke away from the traditional material values of society, and sought to free themselves from the chains of *karma.* They understood the folly of human existence to be man's belief in his separateness from the *atman,* the universal soul, which is veiled and hidden by the ego. They aspired to get in touch with the wisdom inside themselves, to develop compassion and loving kindness, and finally to attain self mastery.

It is a Western view that man is composed of two parts, body and soul, but yoga recognizes that man has three bodies, spiritual, astral, and physical, which are highly integrated. Yogic practices are designed to further perfect this oneness, and to dissolve the feeling of separation between oneself and the universal consciousness.

Several types of yoga evolved as paths for those ardent in the divine pursuit. *Jnana yoga* is self-inquiry, an intellectual approach. *Karma yoga* is the way of selfless service, of work without attachment to its fruit. *Bhakti yoga* uses *asanas,* postures, and *pranayama,* breath control, to stimulate the supernormal power, *Kundalini,* that lies dormant at the base of the spine.

The *Kundalini* energy is naturally present in all human beings and is gradually awakened through the individual's spiritual evolution. By performing *Kriyas,* purification techniques, students cleanse themselves physically before embarking upon the more rigid physical and moral disciplines. These exercises include passing a catheter through the nose and pulling it out of the mouth. *Yogis* following this path strictly adhere to a vegetarian diet.

Through techniques such as these the process of raising the *Kundalini* is speeded up and the energy ascends through the *Shushumna,* the central channel of the astral body, which relates to the physical spinal column. As it ascends the energy passes through the seven power centers or *chakras,* to the crown of the head, where it elevates the consciousness into the state of *samadhi,* supreme bliss, resulting in the absolute union of the astral, physical, and spiritual bodies.

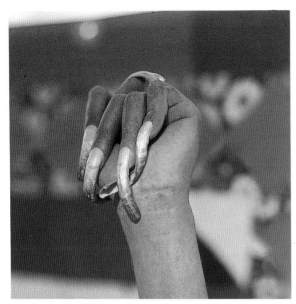

*The fingernails of this ascetic's hand have grown curled around the palm during the four years he has held it upright. Some yogis who undertake this penance grasp rings from the ceiling for support.*

Japa yoga, the repetition of God's name, is considered the simplest method of mind control and purification. Devotees of Shiva believe that His name is so potent, its mere repetition has the power to dissolve sin. Although He has many names, the Sanskrit mantra most often used in the worship of Shiva is *Ohm Namaha Shivaya,* or I bow down to Shiva.

A *mantra* is an invocation to God, or mystic syllables which when repeated, uplift the consciousness. A *mantra* cannot be literally translated, as it is a formula of sacred sound which invokes a deity or state of bliss contained within the actual syllables.

A student is given *mantra* initiation by a teacher who is already familiar with its practice and effects. Yogis believe that the primordial sound *Aum* is the vibration from which all Creation emanates. The power of *mantra* combined with the student's inner force assists in rapid spiritual development. As the divine names are chanted, thought becomes refined and consciousness awakens.

Many seekers endeavour to attain self-realization while living as householders, this path is often called the highest and most difficult. While interacting normally within family and society, they must remain mentally and emotionally unattached, unlike yogis who shun such attachments through avoidance. A popular practice among householders is the singing of devo-

*One of the most difficult austerities a practitioner can attempt is to hold his arm upright in the air for twelve years. It is said that if successfully completed, the practice results in the attainment of supernatural powers. The arm gradually becomes atrophied from lack of use, and with the draining away of fluids it takes on a skeletal appearance and gives the hand a claw - like rigidity.*

tional hymns, *kirtan,* joyfully praising the Lord.

On the other hand some *yogis* attempt to overcome their passions through extreme methods such as celibacy, mortification of the flesh, and denial of the senses. It is written in the scriptures that God realization and powerful supernatural abilities can be attained through austerities. Powers, *siddhis,* such as clairvoyance, levitation and walking on water are considered possible, as is the ability to manifest several bodies at once. *Yogis* whose motivation is to gain *siddhis* do unusual practices such as maintaining silence for years on end, a technique believed to open inert forces within the nervous system.

One austerity, *tapa,* performed to gain powers is that of standing constantly for years. Always

*Offerings are made to a meditator who is buried up to the neck in sand. He supresses the sensations of the flesh while attemping to free his mind through meditation.*

remaining on their feet, these *yogis* even stand while sleeping, by leaning on a padded swing. As they wander from place to place, they remain upright travelling on foot or by train, and often sleep outdoors, by hanging their swing from the branch of a tree.

A few seekers undertake the more arduous practice of standing on one leg only. Due to lack of circulation the limbs sometimes blow up enormously, but usually they return to normal, and when a *yogi* has perfected this technique, he can go on to practice other *tapas*-like holding his

*Lifting enormous rocks with the penis is one of the more unusual ways of desensitizing the sexual organ to overcome lust.*

arm continuously in the air for twelve years. As a result of this difficult practice, the upheld arm becomes atrophied and its fingernails grow black and curled. When some *yogis* initiate this method, they suspend a ring from the ceiling to which their hand can cling.

There are ascetics who pratice two or three austerities at once, such as standing, maintaining silence, and keeping *falahar,* eating only fruit, milk, and vegetables, totally abstaining from grains.

*Siddhis,* supernatural powers are byproducts of

*Accomplished yogis can perform more than eighty difficult asanas, postures.*

*yoga* and not ends in themselves, there is great danger of being seduced by their influence. *Yogis* are cautioned about the pitfalls of power as it can impede further spiritual progress and create more *karma*, binding one further to the cycle of life, death, and rebirth.

Some *Naga babas*, naked ascetics, undergo an initiation in which certain nerves of the penis are broken, making it unlikely they will ever have an erection again. As a prerequisite, the initiate must already have completed nine years of celibacy. Obviously

*Perhaps the most well known austerity is lying on a bed of sharp nails to overcome the limitations of the physical body.*

this rite is extremely painful, and many bribe the initiator to merely act out the ceremony to save face among the other members of their sect. These seekers seem to believe that sexual desire can be extinguished through physical means.

*Yogis* who have not undergone this initiation are known as *Samsara babas,* still caught in the web of human suffering, and are sometimes looked down upon by those who have broken the most fundamental link with human desire - the procreative urge.

The Nagas perform some eccentric exercises such as pulling trucks with their limp male organs, or lifting enormous boulders weighing up to fifty kilos. They tie cloth around a heavy rock, hang it over the penis, and then lift the rock up by grasping the tip of the organ, thereby supporting its full weight.

Although this extraordinary austerity may seem showy, it is practiced to discipline the body and mind. If a *Naga baba* is caught breaking the characteristic celibacy of his sect, he is forced to wear a tight iron ring on his penis in full view of his peers as punishment. These ascetics are referred to as having *kacha langotis,* flimsy loincloths, as they have had sex with women.

Much confusion has arisen from the distinction between *yogis* and *fakirs*. *Fakirs* were originally Moslem street magicians who adopted a few yogic techniques for their repertoires and used them solely for entertainment. Some *yogis* do unconventional practices in sincerity, while unethical ones perform them in public to collect donations and attract the reverence of blind believers. Being buried beneath the sand or lying on a bed of nails captivates the astonished public, while demonstrating the power of mind over matter.

Ascetics who practice unique *tapas* sometimes get lost in the means to the end and lose sight of the end itself. For them, the practice takes priority, the goal is forgotten, and *yoga* is but another crutch of the ego, becoming more subtle as the aspirant continues. Some renunciants take the scriptures literally, practicing austerities such as fasting until emaciated. The true *yogi* seeking union with Shiva goes to no extremes, his mind immersed in God, he follows the path of least resistance, maintaining a conscious remembrance of his divine nature.

The paramount goal of the *yogi* is *samadhi*, the super-conscious state of bliss and tranquility in

*With the assistance of exceptional yogis such as this one, scientific research has documented under laboratory conditions, the ability of some practitioners to hold their breath and go without food or water for extended periods of time.*

80

*In many legends reference is made to Shiva's use of drugs as a means to reach altered states of consciousness. For this reason it is very common to see yogis smoking hashish and using other intoxicating substances.*

which Shiva constantly dwells. During *samadhi* the heartbeat slows and the entire system is at rest, both physically and mentally. Thoughts cease, and the breath can be held indefinitely, the body in a state of total equilibrium.

Some truly unusual *yogis* are able to remain in *samadhi* for several days while underwater or buried beneath the ground, without food, drink, or air. Laboratory tests have been conducted measuring the brain waves of such people while in powerful altered

*Naga babas practice total celibacy to overcome sexual urges. During the initiation into their sect, three vioient strokes are given to their male organs so that they can no longer attain an erection. Such initiates perform exercises with their penises, like lifting stones, stretching and rolling it around a stick, to demonstrate that the nerves have been severed.*

states of consciousness and the results have been remarkable, particularly in the lowering of blood pressure.

*Yoga* has been passed down for eons by ascetics who sought self-realization, renouncing everything to live in the forests and caves of the Himalayas. These men of discrimination, determined to follow the arduous path to self-mastery, have bequeathed to mankind the precious legacy of *yoga*.

# CHAPTER
# XV
## HIS TANTRA

84

*Tantra* is an unortho-
dox path to liberation
through the reconciliation
of opposing forces. Rather
than assuming that passions
do not exist in a spiritual
world, they are accepted as
a source of power and used
to take the *tantrica,* tantric
practitioner, to a higher
level of consciousness. An
important example of this
is the sexual or procreative
drive, which is superseded
only by the self-preservation
instinct.

In *tantra* this erotic
desire is not supressed but
elevated to a point where
sexual union becomes an
exalted state and not just
a mundane act of sense-
gratification. In *tantra,*
conjugal bliss combines the
primordial inactive prin-
cipal, Shiva, and the power
of Shakti, the Great Mother,
merging the two most
vital elements necessary
for liberation.

When the union is
truly complete duality is
dissolved, this mystical
state is heavily interwoven
with erotic emotions. The
boundaries between spiri-
tual and sensual love are
difficult to define, sexuality
contains the germ of both
worldly man and his trans-
cendental self. *Tantricas*
believe that when sense
gratification and ascetic
discipline are coupled
together, they ultimately
conquer the lower nature,
and that desires can be
fulfilled in awareness, not
denied or supressed. The
poison of such passions as
anger and jealousy are
activated and utilized for
spiritual development.

*Ardaneshwar* is ano-
ther of Shiva's manifestations in which the symbo-
lism of *tantric* opposites
is most evident, for *Ar-
daneshwar* is half male,
half female and yet at the

*Tantric motifs depicting sexual poses both erotic and spiritual are common themes in ancient shrines dedicated to Shiva.*

same time one god. As *Ardaneshwar,* Shiva is androgenous, He is portrayed so beautifully, His sexual nature is ambiguous.

One of the many meditative disciplines of *Tantra* is motionless sexual union, using the act of desire as its very conquest. In this *tantric* union, the male moves only enough to maintain his erection, while both members meditate. This lovemaking devoid of lust is a union of ecstasy and discipline, using fulfillment to transcend desire itself. Some *tantric* schools are opposed to the tradition of celibacy, and attempt to

transmute the lower nature through the practice of sexual intercourse.

Shiva's chastity is His divine sexuality. Through asceticism and *tantric* seminal retention, His semen is conserved, swelling His erect phallus with the creative potential of the entire universe, yet He is ever chaste, never spilling His seed. Shiva, the Lord of the Phallus, is both ascetic and sexual, each aspect containing within it the element of the other. In the *Tantra* of Shivaism, Shiva is pure awareness itself, yet not even aware of itself.

*Shiva's androgenous manifestation Ardaneshwar, half man and half woman, expresses the Tantric ideal of perfection in the reconciliation of opposites.*

*Deva-Dasis, or temple prostitutes, exised only in some temples during the height of Tantric popularity.*

Embellishing the many temples of the Hindu world are reliefs which depict couples in sexual embrace, an intermingling of erotic and spiritual symbolism. Consequently, the higher meaning is lost on the casual observer. In some cases this has been deliberately executed to protect the esoteric meaning of *Tantra* from the uninitiated.

As is frequently the case with mystical schools, study under the direction

and guidance of practiced teachers is long and difficult. In the company or brotherhood of fellow seekers, initiations, liturgies and ceremonies are attended which bind the community with a code of secrecy.

At the height of *Tantric* popularity in India, about 8th/9th Cent. A.D., *Brahmin* priests, quick to make the most of a financial opportunity, introduced prostitution into some of the temples, telling the

community that to have sex with their specially gifted *deva-dasis* was a holy act, through which one could receive empowerment.

All of this was possible providing due payment was made to the temple concerned. The *deva-dasis* were originally entertainers gifted in singing or dan-cing, supported by the nobility and the state, and were only later misused by the *Brahmins*. Not all temples were so endowed and most confined their eroticism to the realms of the symbolic only.

The essence of *Tantra* is symbolized by crea-tion and destruction, life and death. The sexual

*In most Tantric temples the erotic was confined to the symbolic only - leaving art whose meaning is today lost on most casual observers*

impulse provides the nourishment for life. Life challenges death, but at the same time offers fresh opportunity for death's insatiably consuming appetite. In death the void is again filled with life and continues on in an endless cycle. The universe is powered by the alternation of these two elemental forces.

*"He who burns his body with the fire of Shiva and floods it with the elixir of his consort by the path of yoga - he gains immortality." Satapath A Brahmana*

# CHAPTER
# XVI
## HIS YOGIS

*Shiva yogis dress in saffron coloured cloth, to symbolize that it has been dipped in the blood of Parvati. Owning few possesions they wander from place to place seeking knowledge and accumulating good karma, while steadily progressing on the path to liberation.*

**Y**ogis follow a path of penance and meditative practices to attain salvation. For thousands of years they have led a lifestyle of total renunciation in the seclusion of India's jungles and mountains, particularly the Himalayas.

Viewing life as *Maya,* an illusion, they reject worldy attachments and seek to merge with the *Atman,* Universal Soul, through simplicity and love, the keynotes of their *Dharma,* truth.

Traditionally a *yogi* first lives with his *guru* for an extended period in asceticism, performing *Karma Yoga,* selfless service while receiving teachings. When his spiritual foundation is strong he begins to wander from place to place, never staying anywhere for long to avoid attachment. It is a saying among renunciants that moving around keeps one clear like a river, whereas staying in one place causes one to become stagnant like a pond. Eventually a hermitage is sought, perhaps a cave, and he retreats into solitude, attempting to reach final union with Shiva.

Devotees of the Lord cover their bodies with ash as Shiva did during His long penance. Some worshippers, *Naga babas,* smear their bodies from head to toe, while others draw three bars in ash on eleven parts of their bodies; across their arms, chest, belly and forehead. Besides emulating Shiva, the wearing of ash is a practical custom, for some *yogis* serving as their only covering in cold climates.

Ashes are worn by *yogis* as a potent reminder of human mortality. A token of humility, ashes are considered to be a pure substance. Aspirants shun clothing to demonstrate that they are no longer susceptible to the passion of lust and remain naked in extreme weather conditions, oblivious to rain, snow, wind and heat.

To ascetics, fire is sustenance and a symbol of Shiva, as they have little clothing and often no shelter, it provides warmth and a cooking medium. The *dhuni,* holy fire, is sacred and building one is the first thing a *yogi* does when he arrives at a new place, whether it be a high Himalayan forest or the roadside of a village. The *dhuni* is carefully dug out, coated with a mixture of water and cow dung, and decorated with flowers. In reverence to Shiva,

*Sometimes female ascetics or yoginis also follow the difficult path of renunciation. Only a few determined women can endure the constant hardships and inevitable harassment which they must often deal with.*

*Kanphatta yogis slit the cartilage of the ear in an intensely painful initiation during which they claim that the astral energy channels are opened to facilitate profound meditation.*

the trident is driven into the ground and the *dhuni* is sanctified. It is kept meticulously clean, no matches, paper, or cigarettes are thrown into it. Some of the most revered shrines are the ancient *dhunies* of saints, which have been kept constantly burning for hundreds of years.

When a pilgrim comes to a Shiva *yogi* for his blessing, a mark of ash from the *dhuni* is placed on the center of his forehead. This *tika*, dot, denotes the third eye and is sometimes multi-coloured and elaborately drawn. Paying homage at a shrine often includes placing a *tika* on the forehead from a paint pot on the altar. Once a demarcation of caste, the *tika* is nowadays merely worn as a cosmetic by many Indian women.

*Chandan*, the three horizontal lines which ascetics draw across their foreheads represents the three impurities they seek to destroy through yogic

practice: egoism, action with expectation of its fruit, and *Maya*, illusion. The markings also stand for the three desires which impede spiritual practice: property, women, and wealth.

Renunciants wear saffroncoloured robes, as their clothes have been symbolically washed in the blood of Parvati, Shiva's consort. At the time of initiation, they shave their heads as a sign of surrender to their *gurus*. Many *yogis* grow their hair back in a *jata*, an unkempt mass, never cutting it again. They rub ash into their locks which become matted and ungroomed to discourage vanity.

Many contemporary *saddhus* seekers, wear ritualistic ornaments such as rhinoceros skin bracelets, believing such objects have the power to liberate one from the cycle of existence. They do not perform yogic practices, but only pay lip service to the ancient traditions. These pseudo-*saddhus* take advantage

*As a yogi moves from place to place, he builds and lives beside a duni, fire pit, which provides warmth and a place to cook. The fire is seen as the light of Lord Shiva Himself and the duni is therefore treated with reverence and kept meticulously clean.*

of the naivety of the uneducated superstitious masses, living off their charity.

In the emulation of their Lord, *yogis* commonly use drugs to reach higher states of consciousness. Shiva, well known to be a notorious lush in many legends, is said to be capable of digesting all poisons. As *Nilekantha,* the blue-throated one, He swallowed the poisons of the world.

*At the time of creation, the Gods churned the great oceans, and fourteen things came out of the water. When nectar emerged, the gods drank it and became immortal, but Shiva was left out. Suddenly poison came from the water, and Shiva drank it, holding it in His neck which turned blue, absorbing the negativity of the world.*

As there are heavy restrictions placed on women by Hindu society, *Sanyasinis,* female *yogis* are uncommon, women find it difficult to leave home and family and become yoginis. Even if they do succeed, they often find restrictions in the company

*Yogis gather around their sacred fire to smoke Hashish while dogs bask in the winter sun. Scavenging dogs are tolerated in cremation grounds by the ascetics who consider them to be messengers of Bhairab.*

*Although other Hindus are cremated at death, yogis are placed in tombs such as these called samadhis. Before being buried their bodies are seated in the lotus posture, cross-legged, and their skulls cracked open so that the spirit may escape through the top of the head, assisting in the passage to a higher rebirth.*

*Shankaracharya, the well known South Indian philosopher, was responsible for the reformation of Hinduism during its decline and the organization of yogis into distinct sects.*

of other *yogis.*

Although Hindus are cremated at death, *yogis* are usually not, their bodies are enshrined in structures called *samadhis,* which means absorption, as death is considered the *maha-samadhi,* or great absorption from the physical world. At the time of initiation into their sect, renunciants perform their own death rites in a fire ceremony, symbolically burning their former lives and egos.

At death a respected *yogi* is seated in the lotus posture facing east or northeast, and lowered into a hole in the ground, where his body is held erect by a wooden frame. The hallucinogenic hemp plant, *bhang,* and a hollow gourd are placed in the grave, and his skull is cracked open in order that the spirit may escape, symbolic of true *yogis* who can willingly cause their spirit to escape through a crevice in the cranium. Devotees build a samadhi above his body and prepare a feast for all the local *yogis,* giving them money and new cloth. The dead bodies of some poor aspirants are simply tied with

*With a compassionate smile and a word of spiritual encouragoment, a Shiva yogi raises his hand in blessing as he places ash on the forehead of a devotee.*

heavy rocks and thrown in the Ganges to sink.

Sometimes burial rites are performed for a living yogi. He is literally buried alive, and is said to be dead only when the ground above him cracks. This "living *samadhi*" is an attempt to leave the body of his own free will in a super-conscious state.

During the decline of Hinduism, Adi Shankaracharya, the great religious reformer, divided India into four sections and appointed a religious figurehead for each. He organized the *yogis* into ten sects to protect the Hindu faith during its decline due to the popularity of Buddhism and Jainism. This monastic

*A guide or guru is essential on the path to enlightenment, but to find a truely realized master is rare. Traditionally the relationship between guru and disciple is mutually demanding. The teacher takes on the responsibility of his disciple's spiritual and sometimes material well being, while the student must show the deepest respect and unquestioning devotion.*

order became known as the *Dashnami Sampradaya*, or Order of Ten Names, these are; *Giri*, hill; *Puri*, town; *Bharati*, learning; *Van*, wood; *Aranya*, forest; *Parbat*, mountain; Sagar, ocean; *Tirth*, temple; *Ashram*, hermitage; and *Saraswati*, perfect knowledge.

The *Dashnamis* are organized in two sections, *Shastradharis*, who are versed in sacred lore, and *Astradharis*, the fighting wing which was divided into *acharas*, sects. During the time of the British Raj, the government recognized the *acharas* and did not interfere with them.

The caste system permeates all aspects of Hindu life, even that of the *yogis*. Certain *acharas*

are exclusive, accepting only *Brahmins* who receive the highest teachings. In contrast, even Moslem mercenaries and low caste Hindus were recruited to join other sects. Wealthy West Indian Maharajas sometimes had as many as ten thousand *Naga Soldier-babas*. With matted unkempt hair and ash smeared bodies the *Nagas*, armed with tridents and swords, stood in the ranks of their armies.

The sects differ in the types of *yoga* practiced and the patron deities worshipped. *Juna Achara* for instance, is said to have more members who have attained yogic powers, than any other sect. This may be because they simply outnumber the other

*Pilgrims sit around fires with the yogis drinking bhang, a drink made from the hemp plant, and smoking chillums of hashish in Shiva's memory.*

*acharas,* or on account of the extreme austerities they practice, such as holding an arm upright for twelve years. The *acharas* established monasteries all over India which provide shelter for *yogis* during their years of wandering.

These monasteries have temples attached which are powerful spiritual centers for the community, and attract donations to support the *achara.* They often have large land holdings and grow cash crops to feed their members and earn additional income.

A *yogi* can perform good works or donate money to his sect, and earn the title of *Mahant,* raising himself in the hierarchy. He becomes responsible for the care and upkeep of the monastery and temple, sometimes overseeing an entire *achara,* and is held in high esteem.

The *Mandaleshwar,* the most learned scholar, holds the place of spiritual leadership in each *achara.*

In addition to the *Dashnami Sanyasis,* other highly unconventional sects of *yogis* have evolved through the Ages.

In Nepal there was a community of Newar *yogis,* from the indigenous ethnic group of the Kathmandu Valley, known as the silent sect. They wandered from village to village begging for alms and rice. These holy beggars smeared their bodies with ash and wore aprons of intricately carved human bone signifying mastery over death.

To attain their fabled powers, these mendicants were bound by custom to maintain silence at all times. They lived on the banks of the holy Bagmati River, a tributary of the Ganges, and slept in the cremation ground. Nowadays these *yogis* are rarely seen, they have lost their traditions being victims of modernization. Members of their caste now work mostly as tailors and only beg once a year as a token of their previous lifestyle.

Shankaracharya was a *Danda Swami,* some of whom lead a remarkably austere lifestyle. They derive their name from the *danda* staff they carry as a token of their vows. Upon initiation they give away all their possessions except a waterpot, loin

102

cloth, and staff.

Cleanshaven and robed in saffron, they dwell in the forests, perpetually travelling from place to place. Even during the excessive monsoon rains, they never seek the shelter of a roof but make their resting place beneath the trees. They subsist only on whatever food is given them, eating it without utensils, directly from their hands. Unlike other *yogis*, they do not light fires but consider them a manifestation of God, to them He is formless.

The Feminine Principle is an important aspect of the *Tantric* school prominent in West Bengal. The *Aghori yogis* worship the Supreme Being as the Divine Mother and believe that through her grace, high yogic powers can be attained.

Although Parvati is regarded as the bestower of life and the nourishing element in nature, she is also worshipped in her fearful aspect as the ruthless destroyer of evil. Her tantric yogis wear leopard skin, which they use as a seat for meditation, in the belief that it protects them from the Earth's magnetic forces. They drink from human skull caps, ritual *tantric* vessels, which signify immortality and the collection of supernatural powers.

*Aghoris* habitually stay in smoky, corpse-ridden cremation grounds, an unparalleled environment in which to overcome repulsion and attraction, and realize the true nature of existence, beyond duality. Sitting beside the funeral pyres, these masters undertake their contemplative pursuits. One initiation they must undergo is eating a morsel of human flesh, given by *guru* to disciple.

The *Nath yogis* follow the path of *Raja Yoga,* the Royal *Yoga,* comprised of both physical and mental disciplines. They worship the 84 *Maha siddhas,* great perfected *yogis* one of which is Guru Goraknath, an embodiment of Shiva and the patron deity of the fierce Gurkha soldiers of Nepal.

*Machendranath, a great yogi, gave some ash from his holy fire to a barren woman, promising her she would soon conceive. In disbelief, the woman threw the ash into a dung heap where sometime later a child appeared. The boy was taken to Shiva, who called him ''Goraknath,'' as ''Ghor'' means filth. Shiva ordered Parvati to cut a large hole in Goraknath's*

*ears as a distinguishing mark.*

Initiates of the Goraknath sect undergo an extremely painful ear cutting ceremony in which the central hollows of the ears are cut with a sharp double-edged knife, and then cork rings are inserted, which have medicinal properties.

Each initiate has a *Kan Guru,* an ear-guru, who while turning the knife in the cartilage, recites the vows of the sect which the initiate must repeat. During the ceremony and for forty days after, the initiate is considered to be Goraknath himself, is kept in isolation, and only allowed to eat butter and milk which is believed to cool the blood.

After nine days, the rings fall out and are replaced by *kundal,* thick clay rings. The initiate is said to have paranormal powers during the period of confinement. After forty days have passed, the *yogi* changes the clay rings for more durable ones of ivory, sandstone, or silver.

In former times, heads of monasteries having large land holdings wore sold gold earrings studded with precious gemstones, the weight of which was supported by a string passed over the head. Some *yogis* wear earrings of snake bone to guard against snake bite. *Kanphatta*, or split-earred *yogis* claim they hear a humming sound constantly while wearing earrings, as the cutting of the ear in this particular spot opens a *nadi,* inner energy channel.

Recently, about two hundred kilometers from Calcutta, the skeletons of five *yogis* dating from eight hundred years ago were found. They were excavated seated in the lotus position with water pots at their sides, still wearing their earrings of clay.

Many snake charmers in India worship Guru Goraknath. Villagers believe these people have the power to bring a human who has died from a snake bite back to life, even if he has died months before-providing that the body has been kept in cow dung. Rather than killing snakes, the charmers render them motionless with a *mantra,* and pick them up to remove them from dwellings.

Through the path of *yoga,* adepts quest for supernatural powers, immortality, and ultimate union with Shiva. He is the greatest ascetic, the Lord of Yogis.

*Some yogis turn showman, while other times it's a showman taking the appearance of an ascetic. The cobras that snake charmers 'charm' are timid, and with little will to bite.*

# CHAPTER
# XVII
## HIS TEACHERS

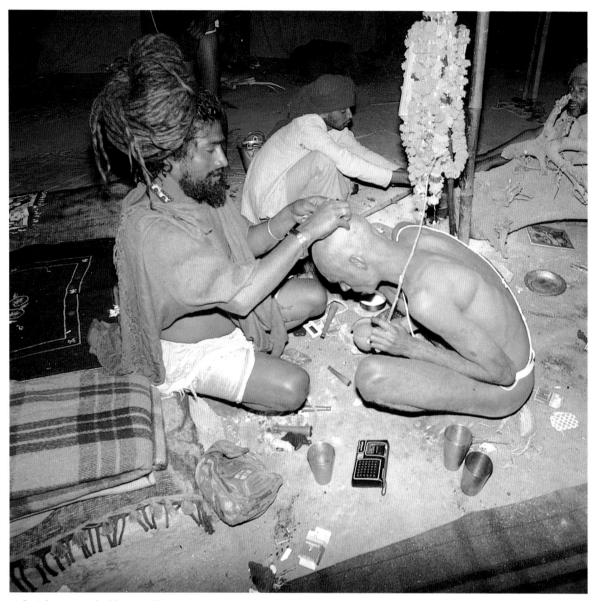

*A disciple receives the blessing of his spiritual teacher after a long initiation ceremony.*

**Y**ogis believe that to progress spiritually, it is necessary to have a guide or *guru* who has already trodden the Path and is familiar with its perils. Some aspirants search endlessly to find their special teacher, while others sense upon the first encounter with their master, the familiarity of many lifetimes, somewhat like a deja-vu experience.

Meeting a true *guru* is a matter of destiny, of ripe *karma*. Hindus believe that one must have performed good actions in one's past lives to be fortunate enough to meet such a pure soul, for if a student is not yet ready, he will not recognize a man of realization even if he comes face to face with him. A seeker must discriminate between marketplace spirituality and a genuine master who is as rare as a precious jewel.

Once the *guru*-disciple relationship has been established, total surrender on the part of the student is of utmost importance, he must develop respect and deep devotion, obey his teacher, and follow whatever *sadhana,* practice, he is given. Reverence is shown to the beloved master by touching his feet, serving

*Prominent gurus are enthroned on elephants and escorted through the streets to bestow blessings on the crowds of expectant pilgrims.*

him, and even shaving one's head. The true *guru* gives guidance and instruction while his disciple develops, confronts his ego, and progresses spiritually.

, As the student becomes more vulnerable, the *guru* acts as a mirror in all situations, reflecting the divine potential within the student. A *yogi* receives initiations and practices from the *guru* designed to unlock his vital energy. The true *guru* never claims he can do the work for his disciple, but shows him the way and guides him with the wealth of knowledge acquired through years of direct practical experience.

The living master is like a receiver through which divine power is transmitted to the student. He acts as a link to the infinite, guiding his disciple through this world and to the one beyond. Some *gurus* are believed to be *avatars*, actual manifestations of God in human form.

It is said that these masters are able to manifest several bodies and appear in many places at once. These teachers have mastered selfknowledge and are no longer limited to the rigid laws of time and space. Their mere presence is uplifting, and their only purpose is to raise the awareness of mankind.

Some teachers offer to connect seekers to the divine through techniques accompanied by a steep monetary fee. Others claim to be God incarnate, displaying powers and miracles attained through *yoga*. A truly realized being would not need to make a business out of his wisdom as his desires would have been transcended and his motivation would be pure compassion.

# CHAPTER
# XVIII
## HIS FESTIVALS

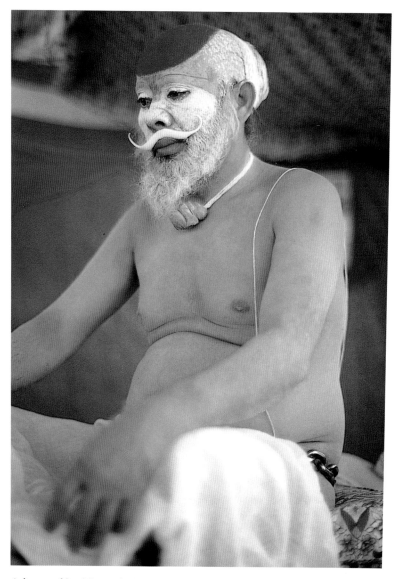

*A devotee of Lord Ram, who has completed twelve years of standing practise, wears the markings of his sect painted on his head in sandlewood paste and vermillion. Around his neck is a Tulsi bead sacred to Ram.*

## Shiva Ratri

The origin of Shiva Ratri, the night of Lord Shiva, is related in a fable.

In ancient times near the City of Light, Varanasi, there lived a violent and cruel hunter. Whilst hunting in the woods one day, he killed so many birds that he had trouble carrying them all home. He grew tired from the weight of his catch and was frequently forced to stop and rest. At last night fell and he was so afraid of being attacked by wild animals that he climbed into a Margosa tree with his catch and prepared to pass the night.

It happened to be the no moon night of the month of "Phalgun," February-March, the night dedicated to Lord Shiva. The hunter spent it hungry, cold and scared to death in a tree. Unknown to him, beneath the tree stood a linga and due to the hunter's frequent changes of position, dew drops, fruit and leaves fell onto it.

Shiva was pleased with these offerings and the hunter's unplanned fasting, as this night was specially consecrated to him. The hunter returned home only to die on the following day. Soon afterwards Yama,

*Pashupatinath in Kathmandu is site of another holy festival to which thousands migrate from all parts of the subcontinent.*

*Looking at himself in a small hand mirror, a pilgrim applies a tika to his forehead. The three verticle lines distinguish him as a follower of Ram, hero of the great Indian epic, the Ramayana.*

*the Lord of Death came to claim his soul, as the man was known to be a great sinner. Lord Shiva intervened for the dead man and told Yama that since the man had fasted and offered sacrifices to the linga on Shiva Ratri night, he had earned his place in Kailash, Shiva's paradise. Thus on Shiva Ratri, devotees, hoping for a place at Shiva's side, keep a similar vigil.*

Shiva Ratri is celebrated all over the Indian subcontinent but the most important centres for this festival are Girnar, situated in the western state of Gujarat, Varanasi and Pashupatinath, the highly revered shrine of Lord Shiva in Nepal.

The forest around Girnar is a powerful centre for meditation, as it is believed to have once been part of the Himalayan range; the jungles, lakes and mountains there shelter thousands of ascetics and during the moon's dark quarter in February-March, the largest celebration of Shiva Ratri is held. According to the local *yogis* the festival has been celebrated in Girnar for at least 500 years.

Throughout the dark night devotees honour Shiva by fasting or eating only fruits and milk. Cries of *"bom Shankar,"* "union with Shiva" are heard, as *chillums,* pipes of hashish, are passed around and offered to the Lord before smoking. *Yogis* and pilgrims

*Tika powders on sale during Shiva Ratri.*

*These devotees of Lord Ram (**above**) have tatooed his name on every inch of their skin and clothing.*
*This shrine atop Guru Shikar peak is the climax of pilgrims' journey during Shiva Ratri (**right**).*

alike share in this ancient ritualistic use of intoxicants in His memory.

Pilgrims come to Shiva Ratri from all over the surrounding areas of Rajasthan and Maharastra erecting tents, giving alms and cooking huge feasts, *bhandaras* for thousands. *Yogis* walk through the villages collecting rice for the feasts to be eaten as *prasad,* sacred food.

The central shrine in the Gir forest area is the majestic Guru Shikar peak, where for countless ages,

saints and sages have meditated, absorbing its intense energy, which is fabled to be a catalyst for spiritual development. Throughout the three days of Shiva Ratri, the entire staircase up to this power spot is lined with throngs of pilgrims for whom the visit to Guru Shikar is the climax of their entire journey.

This is the birthplace of Dattatreya, the three headed manifestation of God, Lords Brahma, Vishnu and Shiva in one body. Thousands of people make the arduous four-hour climb, starting in the early

morning to avoid the ascent in the scorching midday heat. They pay their respects and receive blessings at the numerous shrines along the way, carrying the customary offerings of fruit and flowers, littering the floors of the temples with their devotion.

At the summit of the magnificent peak is the shrine containing the shoes of Dattatreya. It is common in such shrines to find the shoes or footprints of the presiding deity or *guru,* which are worshipped with flowers, fruit, coins and coconuts which symbolize the *yoni.* In Asia, where feet and shoes are considered unclean, it is a sign of deepest reverence to touch the feet of the *guru,* either with fingers, forehead or lips. The view is breathtaking with wide expanses of jungle, and mountains, crowned with a sky of clouds racing into the sunset.

In the lush green valley of Kathmandu in Nepal, lies the ancient temple of Pashupatinath which is consecrated by the relics of Shiva's first wife Sati, whose *yoni* fell there during Shiva's grief stricken wanderings whilst carrying her dead body.

The temple complex is spread along the banks of the holy Bagmati River, which springs from Sivapuri mountain on the rim of the valley and eventually joins the eternally sacred Ganges. The river is believed to issue from the mouth of Shiva himself and is revered by His followers. All along the river banks are cremation platforms, which are in constant use as the devout believe that being cremated there will improve their chances of a higher rebirth.

Surrounding the main temple of Pashupati are many other shrines, homes for the sick and dying who await their fate. On the ghat are shelters for wandering *yogis,* and vendor's stalls selling all kinds of religious memorabilia which pilgrims delight in buying in such holy place.

Within the innermost sanctum, reserved only for Hindus, is the naturally formed *linga* of Pashupati

*An image of the wrathful goddess Kali, enroute by rickshaw to her place of worship.*

which was discovered long ago through the strange behavior of a local cow.

*A herd of cows came everyday to the banks of the Bagmati River to graze. One of the cows developed the peculiar habit of separating herself from the herd to stand on a sandy mound, where she would allow her abundant milk supply to fall upon the ground. Curious about this strange phenomena people decided to excavate the mound and to their surprise and joy, a self-existing or adi-linga was uncovered, and a temple built in its honour.*

Pashupatinath houses the valley's main *gaus-*

*During Shiva Ratri this ascetic moves amongst the crowd collecting rice for communal cookeries. Another devotee in green attends with Shiva's trident and image of the 'king'.*

*hala,* or retirement home for sacred cows which are never killed but given a pension and a place to live out their last unproductive days.

Being one of Shiva's most important shrines, a large Shiva Ratri festival is held at Pashupatinath each year. Many pilgrims travel from India and other parts of Nepal in extremely difficult conditions, to reach Kathmandu in time for the festival.

In the cold wintery dawn the jostling crowd of pilgrims descends on the temple to bathe in the icy river and pay their respects to the great *linga.* Brahmin priests perform elaborate rites to the image. As the priests receive offerings from the devotees they place them on the *linga,* and give in return flower petals and sacred food which has been touched by it. A *tika,* forehead marking, made of sandalwood paste and yellow clay, is then given as a final blessing from the Lord.

Pilgrims are not permitted to touch the phallus as it is said to have magical powers, including the

*Devotees of Shiva dress according to their respective sects (**left & overleaf**) and gather in thousands for Kumbh Mela.*

ability to turn base metal into gold.

As dusk falls the night is filled with the reading of scriptures and the singing of devotional hymns. Multitudes of people wander amid the temples in the forest area, visiting *yogis* to obtain their *darshan,* blessing. Ascetics line the pathways performing their austerities before the astonished public hoping to receive boons from Shiva and donations from the pilgrims.

The aspirants pass the night sitting at their holy fires, smoking *chillums* and drinking huge quantities of *bhang,* an intoxicating drink made from the lower portion of the hemp plant, which they serve from large buckets. It is believed that these intoxicants raise the consciousness. The atmosphere is charged with a mystical exalted quality, as *yogis* keep

*Ascetics march through the town during the festival of Kumbh Mela, while other Naga babas come to the river to bathe enmasse.*

vigil at their sacred fires throughout the night.

Shankaracharya was responsible for the popularization of Saivism in Nepal and allowed many fetishes to be accepted as manifestations of Shiva. The sect of Pashupata, was founded by Lord Shiva himself, when He entered a corpse in the cemetery to pass on His teachings to a chosen devotee. Early observances included simple forms of asceticism, vows of pure speech and action, meditation, and repetition of the *mantra Aum,* to attain union with Shiva.

Later another branch of Pashupatas became popular and called themselves *Kalamukh,* meaning the origin of time. They lived in the cremation grounds, wore a black *tika,* and were predecessors of other lefthand and occult sects, such as the *Aghoris.*

### Kumbh Mela

There is probably nothing more sacred for a devout Hindu than to bathe at a Kumbh Mela, the

123

*During the holy festival Naga babas are initiated in a secret ceremony, during which they perform their own funeral rites. Surrounding the sacrificial fire they symbolically offer their previous lives to the consuming flames, starting life anew as sincere renuciants on the path to Shiva.*

holiest of all festivals; it is held every twelve years during Jupiter's entry into Aries, according to the lunar calendar. At this time, millions of people take the ritual bath in the Ganges, believing that their sins will be cleansed.

As millions of salvation seekers pour into the area, massive tented camps are erected to house the multitudes. Yogis in saffron coloured clothes, villagers, souvenir hawkers, Brahmins and beggars create a carnival-like atmosphere.

There are devotees of Lord Ram from central India, who have tatooed his mantra over every inch of their skin and printed it on their clothes. Beggars are dressed up as Kali, loudly singing for alms. Groups of villagers wearing turbans, cymbals, and peacock feathers wander about the festival rhythmically chanting the marriage song of Shiva and Parvati. People of all castes, and from all walks of life congregate, bound by a common belief.

Seeking eternal life, they flock to the *yogis* for their blessings, believing that their sins will be taken on by the ascetics. They sit with the *yogis* around their holy fires, smoking *chillums* and drinking

tea. Many of the *swamis* only leave their hermitages in the high Himalayas once in twelve years to attend this festival. One side of the river is entirely inhabited by devotees of Ram residing in hundreds of tents, smoke curling into the air from their holy fires. On the other side, scores of Shiva *yogis* hold court in the camps of their *acharas,* while devotional chants and music are blasted over loudspeakers.

Huge feasts funded completely by donations are prepared for thousands. Delicious food is meticulously cooked and equally shared by all as *prasad,* blessed food, in the spirit of giving.

At the auspicious time, thousands of *Naga babas* from all over India, their long, matted hair hanging loosely, armed with swords and tridents, walk in a great procession to the holiest bathing site. The naked ascetics are followed to the river by the *acharas,* warrior *yogis.* Here they cleanse the accumulated sins they carry, and take on the reservoir of sin which has been deposited in the water by the faithful.

Townspeople and pilgrims alike enjoy the spectacle of parading naked saddhus and orchestras

*Most yogis never cut their hair but grow it long and matted to discourage vanity (**above**). They wear little or no clothing, rubbing ash from the fires over their bodies. Naga Babas descend enmasse to bathe in holy waters during Kumbh Mela (**right**).*

escorting *gurus* on elephant back. Floats with en-throned representations of various gods accompany them to the Ganges for a bath in the waters of im-mortality.

During the Kumbh Mela, *saddhus* who are to become *Naga babas,* are initiated in a secret ceremony, which begins their lives anew. Mendicants from all walks of life and ages choose to undertake this diffi-cult path of total renunciation. The initiates take strict vows not to eat more than one meal per day, not to beg from more than seven houses, only to sleep on the ground, not to speak badly of anyone, not to praise anyone, not to bow to anyone except the highest *guru* and only to wear the colour saffron, symbolic of Parvati's blood.

The ritual commences early in the morning, when the initiates shave all the hair on their bodies, after which they take 108 purifying baths in the River Ganges, and cover their bodies in ash. All day they must observe a strict fast and refrain from smoking. Clad only in a loin cloth and blessing string, they carry a staff representing discipline, and a clay cup symbolic of humility, until late in the night when the *Shankaracharya* appears.

After midnight the initiates of each *achara* gather within the camps for their funeral rites. The ritual continues into the early hours of the morning as hundreds of voices sing *''Svaha,''* "so be it," in unison, as fathers, mothers, and all worldly attach-ments are offered into the fire a new life begins. The initiates bathe in the cold river once more. Wet and shivering, they hurry to the holy fires of their respective *gurus* to offer salutations.

The following day thousands of initiates walk barefoot in procession along the flower strewn road in the scorching sun, totally naked, shaven headed, ash covered *Naga babas* at last - His *yogis.*

# CHAPTER
# XIX
## HIS EVOLUTION

*Elements of Shivaism have permeated all aspects of Indian life*

Lord Shiva is to all men all things. His universality and adaptability have preserved His place in the hearts of men for millennia.

The elemental Lord of the Wind, He personified the cataclysmic forces of nature and was the Lord of Destruction. He took on the form of the Cosmic Dancer, His movements creating the ever changing faces of the world.

For the nomadic herdsmen of the Indus Valley, whose primary concern was for the care of their animals, primordial Shiva developed into the Protector of Beasts. Even the Mother Goddess, so revered by the agricultural community, felt His presence and became His consort. The cylindrical symbol, which

*A skeletal demon dances on the wall of Kali's temple, a reminder of human mortality and the proximity of death.*

originally represented the formlessness of Nature, gradually evolved into His phallus and the womb of the Fertility Goddess, its female counterpart. His linga was worshipped as the source of all Creation from which the seeds of existence emanated.

The forest dwelling hermits who renounced society emulated Him as the living Prince of Yogis, the ever vigilant ascetic. When threatened by invasion and religious persecution, He inspired the naked ash-covered mendicants to take up arms for the pre-servation of the faith in His name.

Thus throughout history, the manifestations of Shiva have fulfilled the spiritual needs of a developing civilization. With the dawning of the Space Age, Shiva continues to adapt to the changing circumstances of the world. As primitive belief systems and superstitions quickly vanish, His essence will survive to be worshipped in its purest form, beyond all phenomena, the clear vibrant energy of perfect consciousness.

*Guru Shikar Peak*

# GLOSSARY OF TERMS

| | |
|---|---|
| Acharas | - Sects of Yogis. |
| Aarti | - Hindu ritual offering of light. |
| Asanas | - Yogic postures. |
| Atman | - the universal soul. |
| A-U-M | - the primordial vibration. |
| Babas | - Yogis. |
| Bhakti Yoga | - the path of devotion. |
| Brahmin | - highest of Hindu castes, priestly class. |
| Bhang | - lower portion of the hemp plant, ingested for its intoxicating effect. |
| Chakras | - the seven astral power centers. |
| Chandan | - three horizontal lines worn on the forehead representing the three syllables of A-U-M. |
| Chillums | - clay pipes used for smoking. |
| Damaru | - two - sided finger drum, indicating the feminine and masculine. |
| Danda | - Staff. |
| Deva-dasis | - entertainers, who later became prostitutes attached to certain temples in 8th/9th Century, believed to empower one who has sexual contact with them. |
| Dhams | - four important pilgrimage places in India. |
| Dharma | - Truth. |
| Darshan | - blessing. |
| Dhatura | - hallucinogenic plant from which belladonna is extracted. |
| Fakir | - Moslem street performer. |
| Ghat | - bathing platforms and steps. |
| Gunas | - three qualities of nature. Wisdom and purity; stimulation and passion; inertia and impurity. |
| Guru | - spiritual teacher. |
| Hatha Yoga | - a system of postures and breath control with meditation. |
| Japa Yoga | - repetition of God's name. |
| Jata | - unkempt matted hair. |
| Jnana Yoga | - the path of self-inquiry. |
| Jyoti Linga | - naturally created symbols of Lord Shiva. |
| Kalpa | - Hindu era. |
| Kanphattas | - split-earred yogis. |

| | |
|---|---|
| Karma | - the Hindu law of cause and effect. |
| Karma Yoga | - the way of selfless service. |
| Kriyas | - purification exercises. |
| Kirtan | - devotional hymns. |
| Kshatriya | - warrior caste. |
| Kundal | - thick earrings worn by Nath yogis. |
| Kundalini | - the supernormal power that lies dormant at the base of the spine. |
| Linga | - symbol of Shiva, Creation and His phallus. |
| Mahant | - head of monastery, temple or sect. |
| Mandeleshwar | - most learned scholar of the sect. |
| Mantra | - a formula of sacred syllables. |
| Maya | - illusion. |
| Murti | - an image of god. |
| Nadi | - inner energy channel. |
| Naga | - snake. |
| Om Namaha Shivaya | - a Sanscrit mantra meaning "I bow down to Shiva". |
| Pandit | - Hindu priest. |
| Puja | - worship ceremony. |
| Pujari | - Priest who performs puja. |
| Pranayama | - Yogic breath exercises. |
| Raja Yoga | - the Royal Path composed of mental and physical disciplines. |
| Sadhus | - renunciants. |
| Samadhi | - the ultimate state of incomparable bliss. |
| Samsara | - suffering. |
| Sanyasi | - renunciants. |
| Sanyasini | - female renunciants. |
| Shakti | - Power associated with the feminine. |
| Shushumna Nadi | - central astral energy channel corresponding to the spinal column. |
| Siddhis | - supernatural powers. |
| Sudra | - the laborer caste, sometimes called Harijans. |
| Swami | - yogi. |
| Tantra | - unorthodox path of yoga, using passions to transcend desire itself. |
| Tantrica | - practitioner of Tantra. |
| Tapas | - austerity. |
| Tika | - forehead marking. |

| | | | |
|---|---|---|---|
| Tripundaka | - three horizontal markings on the forehead. | | trinity. |
| Trishul | - Trinity, symbolic of the Hindu | Vaisya | - shopkeeper caste. |
| | | Yoni | - symbol of the vagina. |

# BIBLIOGRAPHY

*Ganga - Sacred River of India*
Raghubir Singh. The Perennial
Press. Hong Kong 1974

*Rati - lila*
Guiseppe Tucci. Nagel Pub. Geneva.
1969

*A History of Religion East and West*
Trevor Ling. Macmillan Press.
London. 1968

*Yoga - A Way of Life*
Ronald Hulchinson. Hamlyn Pub.
London 1974

*The Complete Illustrated Book of
Yoga* Swami Vishnudevananda. Bell
Publishing Co. New York 1974

*Lord Shiva and his Worship*
Swami Sivananda. Divine Life
Society. Teri-Garwhal, U.P. India
1984

*A History of Dashnami Sanyasis*
Dr. Sri Jadunath Sarkar. Pub. by
Sri Panchayati Akhara

*Meditation and Mantras*
Swami Vishnudevananda N.Y. 1978

*Pashupatinath*
Trilok Chandra and Indra Majupurias
India 1981

*Hindu Manners, Customs and
Ceremonies* Abbe Dubois translated
by Henry K. Beauchamp. Delhi, 1981

*Sri Swasthani Brathkatha*
Buddhisagar Paraguli
Ratna Pustak Bhandar

*Siva Purana Vasa*
Pundit Pyarelal Jugu
Labal Kishare Press Lucknow, 1928

*Ancient Indian Tradition and
Mythology* Prof. J.L. Shasti, Ed.
Moti Lal Banarasidas Patna, 1982